Zoom In on
Rocks and Minerals

Minerals

Andrea Rivera

abdopublishing.com

Published by Abdo Zoom™, PO Box 398166, Minneapolis, Minnesota 55439. Copyright © 2018 by Abdo Consulting Group, Inc. International copyrights reserved in all countries. No part of this book may be reproduced in any form without written permission from the publisher. Abdo Zoom™ is a trademark and logo of Abdo Consulting Group, Inc.

Printed in the United States of America, North Mankato, Minnesota
022017
092017

THIS BOOK CONTAINS RECYCLED MATERIALS

Cover Photo: Ido Meirovich/Shutterstock Images
Interior Photos: Ido Meirovich/Shutterstock Images, 1; Sara Winter/Shutterstock Images, 4–5; Albert Russ/Shutterstock Images, 5; Shutterstock Images, 6, 7, 11, 16, 17, 18, 21; Jiri Vaclavek/Shutterstock Images, 8; Brazhnykov Andriy/Shutterstock Images, 9; iStockphoto, 10, 14, 15; Lee Prince/Shutterstock Images, 12–13; Peter Hermes Furian/Shutterstock Images, 19

Editor: Emily Temple
Series Designer: Madeline Berger
Art Direction: Dorothy Toth

Publisher's Cataloging-in-Publication Data
Names: Rivera, Andrea, author.
Title: Minerals / by Andrea Rivera.
Description: Minneapolis, MN : Abdo Zoom, 2018. | Series: Rocks and minerals | Includes bibliographical references and index.
Identifiers: LCCN 2017930310 | ISBN 9781532120459 (lib. bdg.) | ISBN 9781614797562 (ebook) | ISBN 9781614798125 (Read-to-me ebook)
Subjects: LCSH: Minerals--Juvenile literature. | Mineralogy--Juvenile literature.
Classification: DDC 549--dc23
LC record available at http://lccn.loc.gov/2017930310

Table of Contents

Science

Minerals are natural substances. They are all around us.

They make up rocks and other parts of nature.

There are more than 4,000 different minerals on Earth. Salt is a mineral.

Gold is too.

Many types
of minerals
form crystals.

8

Crystals can be different colors.
Some sparkle.

Technology

Graphite is a mineral. It is used to make pencil lead. It is mixed with clay and water.

The mixture is heated.
It becomes hard.
It is then put into pencils.

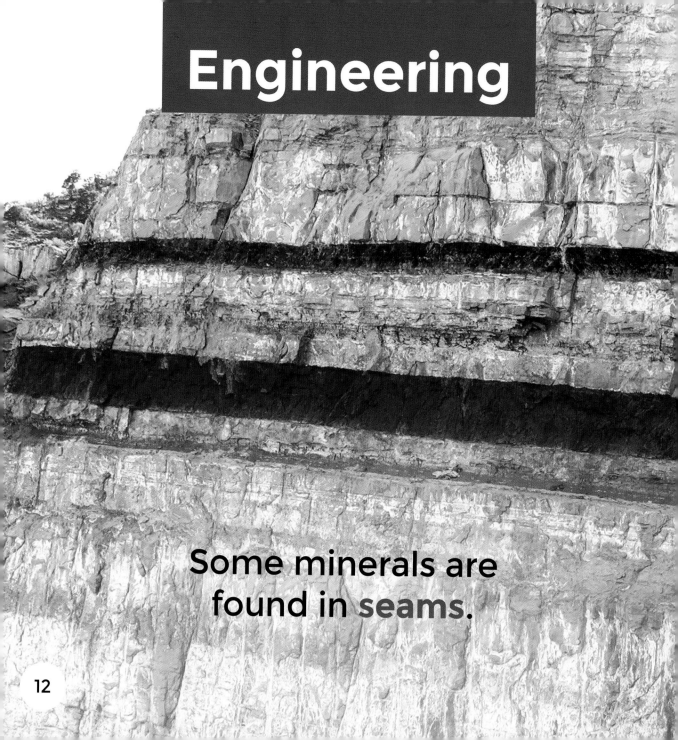

Engineering

Some minerals are found in **seams**.

These can be deep underground.
Humans must **mine** these minerals.

Machines dig a **shaft**. They carve out rooms underground.

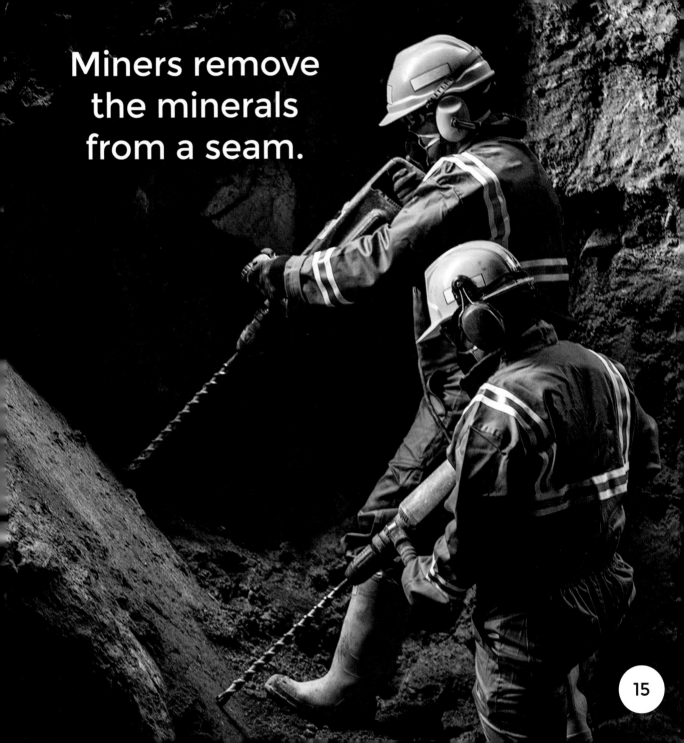

Miners remove the minerals from a seam.

15

Art

Some crystals are used in jewelry. Diamonds begin as dull rocks.

Then they are cut and **polished**.
This shows off their beauty.

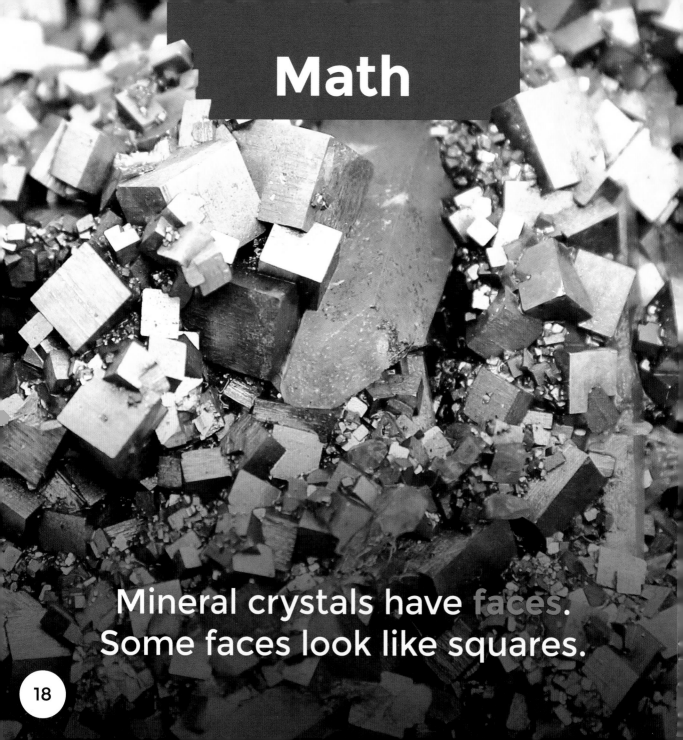

Math

Mineral crystals have faces.
Some faces look like squares.

Others look like triangles.

Key Stats

- Fluoride is a mineral. It is in your toothpaste. Lithium is a mineral, too. It is used in some batteries.

- Water holds minerals. Water can freeze or dry up. Minerals from the water are left over. Halite can form this way. Halite makes salt.

- Some crystals are smaller than a dust speck. Others are bigger than a school bus.

- Diamonds are minerals. They need high temperatures to form. It has to be more than 2,000°F (1,093°C).

Glossary

face - a flat surface that forms the boundary of a crystal.

mine - to dig in earth for metal or minerals.

polish - to rub something to make it shine.

seam - a band of mineral or metal deposits in the earth.

shaft - a long, narrow tunnel that goes straight down.

Booklinks

For more information on minerals, please visit abdobooklinks.com

Learn even more with the Abdo Zoom STEAM database. Check out abdozoom.com for more information.

Index